It's one thing to know an au[thor] and respected counselor. W[hat a joy it is to work] with someone like Heather Nelson and to know the personal stories behind her writing! *Rest* is written by a sincere woman of Christ who is a wise soul-care provider; she's also a close friend of many years who has engaged the struggle we all have to find and cultivate true rest for body, soul, and mind. This devotional book will gently guide you into spacious refreshment in the ways God knows you need.

—**Ellen Mary Dykas**, Author, *Toxic Relationships* (31-Day Devotionals for Life)

Practicing the spiritual discipline of rest can be hard work. Cultural pressures and our own inner critics don't do us any favors with this. So we need experienced guides to help us get there; we need other restless souls who've found rest with the Good Shepherd and who can point us there. Heather has served us well in inviting us to let go of striving and to cultivate rhythms of service and sabbath.

—**Michael Gembola**, Executive Director, Blue Ridge Christian Counseling

Highly personal and full of hard-but-fair self-diagnostic questions, this devotional frames rest as freedom flowing from faith in our Creator rather than as a straitjacket or a burden. Nelson acknowledges that resting well requires effort, but she makes a compelling case that restful refreshment from the Lord is worth it.

—**Alasdair Groves**, Executive Director, Christian Counseling & Educational Foundation

Rest goes on the list of things that are simple (i.e., not complicated) but difficult. Maybe you've read Jesus's invitation "Come to me . . . and I will give you rest" and felt guilty because you feel incapable of unwrapping that gift. If so, Heather takes you by the hand over thirty-one days to help you embrace the rest God wants for you. *Rest* is a book that helps you discipline yourself over a month to create habits that can enrich your life for years to come.

—**Brad Hambrick**, Pastor of Counseling, The Summit Church; Author, *Transformative Friendships*

Speaking as a self-confessed non-rester, I can say Heather Nelson's book was just the tonic my soul needed. Leading with vulnerability and honesty, Heather allows us to walk alongside her in her own journey as she points to Jesus, our true Rest. Each day's devotional brims with hopeful refreshment undergirded by a rich theology of an oft-neglected topic in the church. Read, rest, and be refreshed in the joy of the finished work of our Savior!

—**Jonathan D. Holmes**, Executive Director, Fieldstone Counseling

I love how Heather grounds her exploration of rest in a biblical understanding of the Sabbath. As I finished this devotional, I felt an immense sense of freedom to receive rest as a good and needed gift from the Lord. I recommend this book to anyone who feels weary, tired, burned out, or uncertain about how to incorporate rest into daily life. You will be encouraged and convicted in the best way possible to change your relationship with rest and accept God's good gift of Sabbath.

—**Esther Smith**, Author, *A Still and Quiet Mind*; Licensed Clinical Professional Counselor

R E S T

REST

CREATING SPACE FOR SOUL REFRESHMENT

HEATHER NELSON

P&R PUBLISHING

P.O. BOX 817 • PHILLIPSBURG • NEW JERSEY 08865-0817

Unless otherwise indicated, Scripture quotations are from *ESV Bible*® (*The Holy Bible, English Standard Version*®). Copyright © 2001 by Crossway Bibles, a publishing ministry of Good News Publishers. Used by permission. All rights reserved.

The Scripture quotation marked (NASB) is from the New American Standard Bible® (NASB), Copyright © 1960, 1962, 1963, 1968, 1971, 1972, 1973, 1975, 1977, 1995 by The Lockman Foundation. Used by permission. www.Lockman.org.

Scripture quotations marked (NIV) are from the HOLY BIBLE, NEW INTERNATIONAL VERSION®. NIV®. Copyright © 1973, 1978, 1984 by International Bible Society. Used by permission of Zondervan Publishing House. All rights reserved.

The Scripture quotation marked (NIV 2011) is from the Holy Bible, New International Version®, NIV®. Copyright © 1973, 1978, 1984, 2011 by Biblica, Inc.™ Used by permission of Zondervan. All rights reserved worldwide. www.zondervan.com.

Scripture quotations marked (NLT) are from the Holy Bible, New Living Translation, copyright © 1996, 2004, 2015 by Tyndale House Foundation. Used by permission of Tyndale House Publishers, Inc., Carol Stream, Illinois 60188. All rights reserved.

Italics within Scripture quotations indicate emphasis added.

Printed in the United States of America

Library of Congress Cataloging-in-Publication Data

Names: Nelson, Heather, author.
Title: Rest : creating space for soul refreshment / Heather Nelson.
Description: Phillipsburg, New Jersey : P&R Publishing, [2024] | Series: 31-day devotionals for life | Summary: "Life is tiring, but it's hard to stop hustling! Heather Nelson invites us to explore God's grace to us, discover the holiness of rest, and practice restorative rest in our lives"-- Provided by publisher.
Identifiers: LCCN 2024023703 | ISBN 9781629959801 (paperback) | ISBN 9781629959818 (epub)
Subjects: LCSH: Rest--Religious aspects--Christianity. | Relaxation--Religious aspects--Christianity.
Classification: LCC BV4597.55 .N47 2024 | DDC 242/.2--dc23/eng/20240610
LC record available at https://lccn.loc.gov/2024023703

For Sydney

Thank you for creating space
for me to learn how to rest
through your compassionate presence
and wise counsel

Contents

How to Nourish Your Soul

A LITTLE BIT EVERY DAY can do great good for your soul.

I read the Bible to my kids during breakfast. I don't read a lot. Maybe just a few verses. But I work hard to do it every weekday.

My wife and I pray for one of our children, a different child each night, before we go to bed. We usually take just a few minutes. We don't pray lengthy, expansive prayers. Usually we're brief and to the point. But we try to do this most every night.

What do you see in these examples? Although they don't take long, these practices are edifying, hopeful, and effective.

This devotional is just the same. Each entry is short—just a few tasty morsels of Scripture to nourish your hungry soul. Add it to your daily Bible reading. Read it on the subway or the bus on your way to work. Read it with a friend or a spouse every night at dinner. Make it part of each day for thirty-one days, and it will do you great good.

Why is that?

We start with Scripture. God's Word is powerful. Used by the Holy Spirit, it turns the hearts of kings, brings comfort to the lowly, and gives spiritual sight to the blind. It transforms lives and turns them upside down. We know that the Bible is God's very own words, so we read and study it to know God himself.

Our study of Scripture is practical. Theology should change how we live. It's crucial to connect the Word with your struggles. Often, as you read these devotionals, you'll see the word *you* because Heather speaks directly to you, the reader. Each reading contains at least one reflection question and practical suggestion. You'll get much more from this experience if you reflect on the texts, answer the questions, and do the practical exercises. Don't skip them. Do them for the sake of your own soul.

Our study of Scripture is worshipful. Are you weary because of the frantic pace of your life? Maybe you feel like there's too much to do and you never get a proper break. Every weekend, you run to your typical refuges—streaming video or sleeping late on Saturday morning. It's good to take a break, but you don't emerge truly rested. These substitute refuges don't fully deliver on their promises. Dig a little deeper, and you find obstacles to rest in your own heart. Unbelief and a blindness to God's goodness serve as barriers. What can you do? Where can you find the rest that you need?

This is why God's Word matters. You need a Savior who is merciful and long-suffering toward your weary soul. You can't find true rest on your own. Jesus invites you, "Come to me." What does your study of the Word lead you to? Worship of him. Christ reminds you, "I can give you rest." Every time you feel exhausted, it's a reminder that you can't survive this life on your own—you need Jesus to help you. You look to a Savior who offers a compassionate word as he invites you to find true and lasting rest. As you study your Bible, you will learn that God has a lot to say about rest. He offers you a more restful life this side of death and, even more, an eternal rest in glory.

If you find this devotional helpful (and I trust that you will!), reread it in different seasons of your life. It will help remind you of God's goodness and power and promises whenever you desire rest. So work through it this coming month, and then come back to it a year from now, to remind yourself about what God and the gospel teach us about cultivating a life of true rest.

This devotional starts you on a wonderful journey that will help you find more rest for your life. After you finish reading (and rereading) it, if you want more, you'll see more resources listed at the end of the book. Buy them and make good use of them.

Are you ready? Let's begin.

Deepak Reju

Introduction

REST? MAYBE YOU love the concept but have a hard time putting it into practice. Perhaps you're in a season of life when the demands on your time have increased and rest seems like an unrealistic luxury. Or maybe you've been immersed in a difficult calling, whether ministering to others, caring for an aging parent, raising young kids, leading a company, or a combination of the above. Rest feels elusive. You aren't sure how you'll find the strength to keep loving and serving.

We live and serve in a weary world. Life is tiring, and rest is far too often a luxury. Throughout Scripture, God invites his people to rest so that we can live truly fruitful lives that we lay down in love for others. Yet not only does he invite us to rest, but he also empowers us to rest through the Holy Spirit who indwells us.

Throughout our time together in this devotional, we'll explore the exact nature of the rest that God invites us to enjoy (see Ex. 20:8–10; Ps. 62:5; Heb. 4:9–10), investigate why rest is holy (see Gen. 2:3), and learn with Mary about what "one thing is necessary" (Luke 10:42). Most importantly, we'll figure out how to practice rest in a way that is uniquely our own. As we transform our perspective, our pace, and the pattern of our days, we will become not only hearers of the Word but doers as well (see James 1:22–25).

A change of *perspective* means learning to rest and abide in Christ instead of pursuing a works-based salvation. A change of *pace* comes from trusting God and resting in him to provide instead of hurrying and hustling out of worry and fear. Finally, a change of *pattern* means setting aside regular hours, days, and weeks to rest from our usual labor.

My Story: Burnout and the Absence of Rest

In 2016, I found myself in a season of vibrant ministry on all fronts. The publication of my first book was bringing long-held desires to fruition, I had speaking engagements around the country and a busy and full counseling ministry at a local church, and all the while I was raising energetic preschool-aged twins and investing in the women's ministry of our church. In the middle of this very fruitful period, Deepak Reju called to ask me about contributing to the 31-Day Devotionals for Life series. Everything in me wanted to say yes, but I had begun a downward spiral that was propelling me into a dark season of burnout and depression.

There was a crucial element missing from my apparently fruitful ministry, and that was rest. I had yet to learn the habit of rest, nor did I understand my freedom to rest in the *finished* work of Jesus. My theology proclaimed Jesus Christ's all-sufficient work of salvation, but I lived with an inward pressure to work harder and produce more, unwittingly attempting to add to Jesus's redemptive work in my church, my family, and my community. I fell apart as I lived under the weight of a heavy yoke I was never meant to bear. After failing to heed the warning signs, I arrived at a place physically, emotionally, and spiritually where I was unable to do anything but the most basic activities for daily life.

As God pruned away what I considered to be "my fruit," I learned anew how little is required to abide in Jesus as he holds me with grace and love. I learned that Jesus's yoke is easy and his burden is light. Friends and relatives surrounded me, cared for me and my family, and helped to ease us back into wellness. Now I work as a part-time biblical counselor and writer, manage our home, and parent our adolescent daughters. I rest more regularly, though not perfectly, and I'm just now—six years later—engaging in this writing project.

God met me in a difficult season and taught me to trust him more as I learned the beauty of rest. He invited me and drew me to come to him for true rest—soul rest that came through physical and emotional rest too. This wife-mom-counselor-writer-speaker-friend is learning the value of weekly and seasonal periods of rest, the importance of saying yes and no in ways that honor the boundaries God has given me, the joy of restorative sleep and regular physical exercise, and the refreshment of a good old-fashioned afternoon nap. I hope and pray that in our thirty-one days together, you'll join me in laying down the heavy burdens you're carrying as we come to Jesus for true rest.

How to Read This Devotional

How can this devotional be most helpful to you? Simply reading the material for each day will have some value in your life, for God's Word never returns void and always accomplishes the purpose for which God sends it (see Isa. 55:10–11). And yet Scripture teaches from beginning to end that God's Word is never intended *only* to be read and ingested. Its purpose is to equip us "for every good work" (2 Tim. 3:17). Don't read this devotional without also committing to implement rest in your life. Use the practical suggestions at the end of each meditation to make a start by putting its lessons into practice.

If I were sitting across from you in my counseling office or over a cup of coffee, I'd lean in and tell you that *small beginnings can produce big change.* Think about faith the size of a mustard seed, which Jesus proclaimed was enough to move a mountain (see Matt. 17:20). When I was a mom of newborn twins, I wanted to observe a weekly day of rest. All I could come up with was to take a break from doing laundry on Sundays. And here's the thing: God, who sees what's done in secret, who knows the direction of your heart, will multiply even the smallest decisions such as these. So, even right now, take one minute to settle your heart, take a deep breath, and pray for God to remove whatever hinders rest in your life.

Here's a brief overview of where we're headed in this devotional:

- We'll begin by looking at *what rest is* in days 1 through 10, seeking to define a biblical pattern and practice of rest. Here we'll see the significance of the Sabbath in particular.
- In days 11 through 22, we'll turn to the next practical question that arises: *how to rest*. In this section, we will examine how to appreciate the gift of sleep, how to exchange our burdens for Jesus's easy yoke, and how to turn away from what hinders rest. We'll see that God's compassion welcomes us to the rest we need.
- Finally, we'll meditate on *where to rest* in days 23 through 31. As we conclude, we'll see that all our rest foreshadows the eternal rest that awaits us with Christ in heaven.

Are you ready to begin? Let's say yes to Jesus's beautiful invitation to rest and trust him more fully and deeply to produce his good work through us as we rest and abide in him.

> Come to me, all who labor and are heavy laden, and I will give you rest. Take my yoke upon you, and learn from me, for I am gentle and lowly in heart, and you will find rest for your souls. For my yoke is easy, and my burden is light. (Matt. 11:28–30)

WHAT IS REST?

DAY 1

The Beginning of Rest

And on the seventh day God finished his work that he had done, and
he rested on the seventh day from all his work that he had done. So
God blessed the seventh day and made it holy, because on it God
rested from all his work that he had done in creation. (Gen. 2:2–3)

EXCELLENT STORIES HAVE compelling beginnings. The
story God tells in the Bible, from Genesis to Revelation, has a *very*
good beginning. There is nothing, and then there is everything.
Over six days, God speaks the entire cosmos into being—it is the
most productive workweek imaginable. But what happens next is
striking. God stops. Into his pattern of daily work, he weaves an
entire day of rest. It's a holy pause.

Did God stop because he was tired? The work of creating an
entire universe exhausted him, and he needed to catch his breath?
Absolutely not. This is the God who needs "neither slumber nor
sleep" (Ps. 121:4), who is all-powerful and all-creative, who pos-
sesses a well of infinite resources and strength from which to draw
for all eternity. No, God rested because he knew the creatures he
had made in his image—including you and me—would need rest.

Adam and Eve, the first humans, were given the work of tending
the garden of Eden and stewarding all God had made. Even before
sin brought futility and frustration into their work, God gave them
a day of rest to replenish and refresh them. It was to be a holy pause
in which they could remember and worship the God who provided
for their every need—even, and *especially*, their need for rest.

As we begin to define rest, we consider the purpose of the
very first rest. God's rest was the cessation of "his work that he
had done" (a phrase repeated for emphasis three times in these
two verses). It signaled an end to his work of creation.

But we also see that God's rest established a pattern of rest for his creatures. God is infinite; we are finite. *God* didn't need to rest: God chose to rest, knowing that *we* would need to rest. We worship a God who knew we would need to take breaks from our work.

What work fills this season of your life? A job may be the first thing that comes to mind, but work isn't limited to paid employment. Work is anything you do with some degree of necessity that involves your sustained effort. This may include studying in school, managing your home, tending your land or yard, parenting children, caring for your parents or your spouse, and volunteering in your church, school, or community. What will your rest be? At its simplest, rest is pausing from this work.

Reflect: What pattern did God establish for work and rest in the creation week?

Reflect: Consider the difference between you as *creature* and God as *Creator*. How is God's day of rest a gift to his creation?

Act: Define your work during this season. What is requiring your effort?

DAY 2

Rest Is a Mark of Freedom

And God spoke all these words, saying, "I am the LORD your God, who brought you out of the land of Egypt, out of the house of slavery. . . . On [the seventh day] you shall not do any work." (Ex. 20:1–2, 10)

WHEN ADAM AND EVE disobeyed God's good command, the pattern of work and rest he had set for them was disrupted. Sin, death, and futility entered the world, and work became painful and difficult (see Gen. 3:17–18). Now, in the book of Exodus, God explicitly lays down the pattern once more. Six days of work are to be followed by one day of total and intentional rest.

Consider the context in which God restores this pattern. He has just miraculously rescued the people of Israel from centuries of slavery under harsh Egyptian taskmasters. Shortly before their escape, Pharaoh had increased their workload so that it was impossible for them to meet their work quotas (see Ex. 5:16). He had no intention of allowing his slaves to snatch physical rest.

Now God reassures his people, whom he has rescued from bondage, that he will be a very different king over them. The commandments he gives them are part of their "freedom charter."[1] For these freed slaves, a day of rest is a welcome relief. Rest is something they *get* to do.

God's people experienced an even greater exodus when God, through Christ, rescued us from our slavery to sin. If rest was part of the Israelites' freedom charter, how much more so is it to be part of ours? Rest is a mark of the freedom we have as God's people. I'm convicted of the many times I've complained that I have "too much to do" when offered an upcoming day or season of rest. We wear "busy" like a badge to indicate our worth, when the reality is that it's a chain that is keeping us enslaved.

Freedom to rest isn't only for your individual benefit. Yes, you have been rescued from slavery to sin through God's grace, and meditating on this spiritual reality will bring you much joy and rest. But no party is complete without other people. We are to extend the grace of rest to those in our households, those in our workplaces, those passing through our communities, and even the livestock that labor in our fields. This is comprehensive, because our freedom is meant to overflow into a large-scale community-wide rest. I don't know what this will look like for you, but I invite you to consider together with your community how to experience and extend rest out of a heart that rejoices in our collective freedom.

Reflect: Think about rest as a mark of your freedom. How might that change your attitude to rest and the way you pace your days?

Act: Make a list of all those in your home and workplace. How could you invite them to rest? In what ways could you free them to rest? (For example, as a parent, consider not requiring chores for your kids on Sundays, or, as an employer, consider not expecting communication from employees on their days off.)

DAY 3

The Priority of Sabbath

"Remember the Sabbath day, to keep it holy. Six days you shall labor, and do all your work, but the seventh day is a Sabbath to the LORD your God. On it you shall not do any work." (Ex. 20:8–10)

TODAY'S PASSAGE WAS WRITTEN to the Israelites as they journeyed from Egypt to the promised land. In it, God establishes a day of rest for his people called the *Sabbath day*. It is an echo of creation's order. Because God rested from his creation work on the original Sabbath, we too are to rest fully from our work one day out of every seven.

The command to observe the Sabbath is the fourth of the Ten Commandments found in Exodus 20:1–17. It's the hinge commandment that transitions from commands for honoring God to commands for honoring neighbor. The order communicates God's priorities. For us to honor him as God above all others (see Ex. 20:1–6), we must remember the Sabbath and pause from our labor for one day a week. In resting from our work, we remember that we creatures are not God, and we find strength in God to obey his commands to love our neighbors (Ex. 20:12–17).

I've never heard a Christian argue that honoring parents, abstaining from murder, or refraining from idol worship is irrelevant today. But Sabbath observance? We often see it as legalistic—a relic of the Old Testament law that's been replaced by Jesus's law of grace. I wonder if that's because this commandment offends our Western productivity culture more than any other. Many think it's inconvenient, unproductive, or just unrealistic to keep a whole day of rest.

In the agrarian culture in which the Israelites lived, not tending the land for a day could have a potentially irreversible impact.

When it was harvesttime, it was "all hands on deck" all day, every day. But God commanded his people to rest even during these times—and not only his people but also their servants, livestock, and guests. By doing this, they set apart the Sabbath from other days and kept it holy.

Sabbath rest isn't optional for God's people. It has been commanded by God, whose holiness and steadfast love are magnified through our Sabbath remembrance. His commands are not burdensome—they are meant to bring life. No other religion or god calls us to worship by ceasing from our work rather than by adding to our burdens. When we rest from the work that consumes the other six days of each week, we are re-created and refreshed. God's goodness shines in the gift of Sabbath rest.

Reflect: Have you treated the fourth commandment as optional? Why or why not?

Reflect: What benefits might Sabbath rest bring not only to you individually but also to your community?

Act: God doesn't command what his grace won't supply (see 2 Cor. 9:8). Where will you specifically need grace to observe the Sabbath day this week? Ask God for this grace, and then take a step of obedience this Sunday.

DAY 4

The Sign of the Sabbath

"You are to speak to the people of Israel and say, 'Above all you shall keep my Sabbaths, for this is a sign between me and you throughout your generations, that you may know that I, the LORD, sanctify you.'" (Ex. 31:13)

A SIGN POINTS to a reality. Throughout God's long relationship with his people, he gave them signs to represent his promises to them. One of the most well-known is the sign that God gave to Noah and his family after he rescued them from the flood (see Gen. 9:12–17). When they tiptoed off the ark onto dry ground after more than a year of seeing nothing but the water that had wiped out the world they knew, God used a rainbow to remind them of his promise not to send another flood to destroy the earth.

God also gives his people signs to signal his covenantal relationship with them. These signs are reminders that they belong to him. For Abraham and his descendants, circumcision was a tangible sign that the Israelites were set apart for God (see Gen. 17:9–13). After God miraculously rescued his people from slavery in Egypt, he gave another sign by instituting the annual Feast of Unleavened Bread to remind the Israelites and their descendants of what he had powerfully done for them (see Ex. 13:3–10). In later instructions to Moses, God gave yet another sign: the Sabbath day.

What greater realities does this particular sign indicate? First, as we see in today's passage, it is a sign that the Lord is the one who sanctifies his people. As we'll see more explicitly tomorrow, it also demonstrates that his people are in an eternal covenant with him (see Ex. 31:16) and reminds us that the Lord rested and was refreshed on the seventh day of creation (see v. 17). Did you realize that Sabbath observance means so much?

When you and I practice Sabbath-day rest as God's people, we are signaling nothing less than the reality that our holiness comes from the Lord who created heaven and earth. In keeping the Sabbath day, we are proclaiming that we're sanctified *not by our own work* but by God's work in us and for us. God's people kept the Sabbath day through many generations, pointing to an eternal covenant.

God's promise to sanctify his people was ultimately fulfilled by Jesus Christ. Israel's Sabbath-day observance pointed forward to the reality that the holiness of Jesus Christ would become ours. In the same way, our Sabbath-day observance today points back to our rescue through Jesus Christ. This day of obedient rest signals to the world around us that we are chosen by God to be his own people. It's one of the unique ways that God's people are marked as his own, distinct from the peoples and cultures and nations around them. No other "god" says that *resting* is a mark of belonging. Because God is the one who sanctifies us, we are free to rest and be refreshed each Sabbath day.

Reflect: What's something new that you learned about the sign of Sabbath observance for God's people?

Act: Think of a way to practice Sabbath-day rest that reflects what you learned today.

DAY 5

Sabbath Rest Is Refreshing

"The people of Israel shall keep the Sabbath, observing the
Sabbath throughout their generations, as a covenant forever.
It is a sign forever between me and the people of Israel that in
six days the LORD made heaven and earth, and on the seventh
day he rested and was refreshed." (Ex. 31:16–17)

WHEN WE THINK about "observing the Sabbath," we might
call to mind scenes from the *Little House on the Prairie* series in
which naughty Laura Ingalls Wilder gets scolded by Pa for going
sledding on a Sunday. However, the description of a day of rest in
Exodus 31 is quite different from the dour Sabbath observances
Wilder endured. Notice how God's first Sabbath is described in
this passage: "He rested and was refreshed."

In day 1, we defined rest as "pausing from work." Now let's
add what we are to do *during* that rest: we are to pursue refreshment. To be refreshed is to have your strength restored as you
renew your supply of energy.[1] I love my friends' definition of
refreshing rest: "Rest comes through the patient practice of which-
ever activities refill and recharge our minds, bodies, and spirits to
do the good work God has called us to do."[2] Rest ought to bring
us physical, emotional, and spiritual refreshment as we practice it.

The Sabbath is our primary and most extensive opportunity
to practice this kind of rest. Worship with a local church body
reorients our souls and minds to the goodness and beauty of
God and his people. In addition, my own family has embraced
the Sunday afternoon nap. Our bodies are reinvigorated through
this time of extended sleep, and so also our minds and souls are
renewed to face whatever the workweek ahead holds for us.

As you think about how to make Sabbath rest refreshing, what other activities come to mind? A long hike in the woods or through a park is holistically refreshing. Reading a good book can also refresh the mind and soul. Enjoying a meal with friends or family refreshes our spirits, minds, and bodies.

As you plan for the Sabbath and for other periods of rest, consider which activities "refill and recharge your mind, body, and spirit." What is a refreshing contrast to how you spend most of your time? For example, if you work at a desk job, refreshment for you will likely include physical activity—ideally outdoors in the fresh air. If you're with people, big or little, most of your week, solitude will likely be an important aspect of refreshing rest for you. As you cease from work and engage in life-giving activities and practices in a weekly pattern of Sabbath rest, you will find refreshment *from* and *in* your rest.

Reflect: When have you been refreshed by Sabbath rest—by taking one day a week to cease your work and focus on rest?

Act: Look at how you defined your work on day 1. Now make a list of activities that you find to be refreshing. Consider what refreshes you mentally, physically, and spiritually, as well as what is a contrast to how you spend your time and energy most days. Practice incorporating one of these refreshing activities into your Sabbath day of rest.

DAY 6

Sabbath Rest Is a Delight

"If you turn back your foot from the Sabbath, from doing your pleasure on my holy day, and call the Sabbath a delight and the holy day of the Lord *honorable; if you honor it, not going your own ways, or seeking your own pleasure, or talking idly; then you shall take delight in the* Lord, *and I will make you ride on the heights of the earth." (Isa. 58:13–14)*

God established his Sabbath as part of his covenant with the people of Israel, but their hearts soon hardened, and they drifted away from him to worship other gods. One expression of their disobedience was the way they began to misuse Sabbath rest. Ironically, the people used the Sabbath day to seek their own pleasure, and in pursuing pleasure on their own terms, they missed out on true delight.

What's the difference between *pleasure* and *delight*? We see in today's passage that *pleasure* reflects a self-centered pursuit of happiness or distraction, while *delight* comes from centering our joy on God. Worldly pleasure is an *escape* from our lives that diminishes or weakens our souls. In contrast, God-honoring delight enriches our souls in a way that renews and restores us to better *engage* our lives.

Like Israel, we need to turn away from some of our default pleasures and self-centered escapes or at least rethink how we engage in these activities.

Consider the difference between enjoying dessert as a fitting conclusion to a nourishing meal and skipping dinner to binge eat a carton of ice cream. Which approach leaves you feeling guilty? Which yields the most pleasure and appreciation for the sweet treat itself? Eating ice cream isn't the problem in the second scenario; the problem is elevating the dessert to meal status and missing out on the larger good of a balanced plate. Having fun is not prohibited as long as we honor God. On the Sabbath especially, our activities shouldn't exclude a chance to rest.

How can we ensure our delight is God-centered instead of self-centered? Consider the words of missionary Amy Carmichael (penned long before social media, smartphones, or video streaming services): "'[There is no harm in recreation] if by recreation is meant *re-equipment for future work with no leakage of spiritual power.*' We must have a fresh influx of life for both soul and body, or we shall dry up and become deserts in a desert. But where are our fresh springs to be? . . . 'All my fresh springs are in Thee.' . . . Can we say so truthfully?"[1]

As you finish today's reading, consider the impact your recreations have on your mind, body, and soul. Do they leave you feeling energized and encouraged—or worn out, regretful, or even guilty? What activities or pursuits—even those that may not seem particularly spiritual—refresh your heart in the Lord? As you turn away from self-centered recreation, pleasure, or entertainment, you will be freed to find deeper streams of true delight.

> **Reflect:** What's the difference between self-centered entertainment and God-glorifying delight? List a few examples in your life for each category.
>
> **Act:** During your next day of Sabbath rest, consider which activities will help to realign your heart to delight in the Lord and yield spiritual refreshment.

DAY 7

The Priority of Physical Rest

*[Elijah] sat down under a broom tree. And he asked that he might
die. . . . And he lay down and slept under a broom tree. And behold,
an angel touched him and said to him, "Arise and eat." And he looked,
and behold, there was at his head a cake baked on hot stones and a jar
of water. And he ate and drank and lay down again. And the angel of
the LORD came again a second time and touched him and said, "Arise
and eat, for the journey is too great for you." (1 Kings 19:4–7)*

EMMA SLUMPED WEARILY on the couch in front of me. As
she poured out her emotions, a theme emerged. She was tired, so
very tired. She faced the relentless demands of parenting as well
as caring for an aging parent who'd recently moved into her home.
She was worried about her teenage son's mental health and at
times felt like she shouldn't leave him on his own. Her husband's
job took him away from home for frequent travel, and she felt
alone as she tried to meet the needs of the household. Depressed
and anxious, she couldn't concentrate to pray or read her Bible,
and she'd fallen out of touch with her church community group
as her family's needs increased.

Where should I begin as her counselor? Should I encourage
her to go to church more frequently, to be more consistent in
small group and in her daily devotions? In today's passage, notice
how the Lord responds to the prophet Elijah when he becomes
so frightened and weary that he wants to die. The Lord's initial
response to Elijah is to tenderly meet his physical needs. An
angel delivers water and freshly baked food, not once but twice.
The Lord knows what is in Elijah's past and future, and he knows
the journey is "too great" for him without physical nourishment
and rest.

In my first meeting with Emma, we talked about how to care for her physical body while caregiving for others. Prioritizing physical rest would help her to clarify what steps to take next. She set the goal of getting seven to eight hours of sleep each night and developed a bedtime routine that would help her unwind after each day. We talked about how to incorporate healthy meals and snacks into each day and discussed the possibility of receiving meals from her church community, who longed to do something practical to support her. We also identified a few mental breaks she could take throughout her day, as well as opportunities for physical exercise.

It was hard for Emma to accept some of this advice because it didn't feel "spiritual." But when I took her to this passage, she teared up as she saw the Lord's tender, practical care for Elijah's physical and emotional weariness. Although spiritual considerations are important and must be addressed, remember that God knows our frame, and he has compassion on us (see Ps. 103:13–14). He offers physical rest to his weary children.

Reflect: Are there physical needs that you've been neglecting? Consider sleep, meals, and exercise as a starting point.

Act: Put aside time today for a physical pause from your work—perhaps a nap or a walk, a conversation with a loved one, a more intentional mealtime, or an earlier night.

DAY 8

An Invitation to Busy Disciples

*The apostles returned to Jesus and told him all that they had done
and taught. And he said to them, "Come away by yourselves to
a desolate place and rest a while." For many were coming and
going, and they had no leisure even to eat. (Mark 6:30–31)*

JESUS'S KINDNESS AND compassion for his disciples pours
forth in our brief passage for today. They're thrilled to tell him
about their ministry ventures. He listens, and then he invites
them to do what they need at that moment: not to engage in more
ministry but to rest.

I doubt that the disciples complained of being tired. In fact,
they seem energized and exhilarated as they describe all that they
saw God do through them. But Jesus—God made flesh, their
Creator—knows that they need physical rest away from their
ministry context, even if they are tempted to resist it. After all,
they've been so busy they haven't even had time to eat! (If you're
a parent at home with little ones, doesn't that sound familiar?)

Today's passage again reinforces why God set aside an entire
day for rest at the beginning of creation. We humans need to be
replenished on a regular basis. Especially after busy, even fruitful,
seasons of work and ministry, we are to heed Jesus's call to "come
away . . . and rest a while." On the Sabbath day, we feast on rest
by refreshing our souls, bodies, and minds—practicing the rest
that we'll need to enjoy in less concentrated form throughout the
week as well.

Rest happened *before the fall*. Not only do our souls need rest,
but our bodies need rest too. We were created not only to work
but first to rest. The fall flipped this paradigm with sin's deceit-
ful whispers that we must work to prove our worth, that we can't

afford to take time for adequate sleep or a day of rest. Jesus came to restore us, showing us by his own life that we are free to rest and inviting his disciples to do so too.

In coming away to be with Jesus more intentionally on the Sabbath day, we are reminded anew that we are not limitless—only God is—and that he is the source of our strength. The practice of regular Sabbath-day rest overflows into a posture of rest through-out the week and after busy seasons of ministry. These pauses are times to heed Jesus's invitation to check in with him, talking to him about our work and ministry and receiving from him what-ever we need to keep going. We may need a particular passage of Scripture, a phone call or text to a friend to ask for wisdom and support, a quick walk outside to gain energy and perspective, or a nap. Rest is spiritual, but it is also physical. Jesus knows how we are made (see Ps. 103:15–17). He has compassion, reminding his disciples—and us—that we need physical rest in order to be revived spiritually for the work we are called to do.

Reflect: Do you think of rest as being as essential to your phys-ical well-being as food and water? What physical cues indicate that you're tired and need to rest? Do you tend to pay attention to these cues or to ignore them—and why?

Act: Begin to honor your body's need for physical rest by try-ing to get enough sleep, as much as your current life season permits. If your nighttime sleep is interrupted, make time for a nap during the day. The ideal is anywhere from twenty to ninety minutes.[1] If daily naps are hard to incorporate into your routine, try taking a weekly Sunday afternoon nap (or find another day that works better for you).

DAY 9

A Spiritual Posture

My soul finds rest in God alone; my salvation comes from him. He alone is my rock and my salvation; he is my fortress, I will never be shaken. (Ps. 62:1–2 NIV)

EVER SINCE THE snake slithered into Eden and left sin in its wake, we've been living in a fragile world. Although we look for safety and security, we are always disappointed. Routine medical appointments deliver life-altering diagnoses. Accidents take away loved ones without a goodbye. The possessions we work so hard to obtain and maintain are stolen or destroyed. Disasters and pandemics devastate the globe. Meanwhile, sin taints every relationship we will ever have, and some relationships break under its strain.

Only God provides a security that cannot be taken away, though we lose our earthly possessions, our relationships, and even our very lives. The author of today's psalm knew this well. King David was hunted for years by Saul; for years he had lived on the run, hiding in caves along with his tribe of distressed, indebted, and bitter men (see 1 Sam. 22:2); he committed dire sins against God and others (see, for example, 2 Sam. 11); and he lived to see at least three of his sons die—one at the hands of his brother.

Yet David is called "a man after [God's] own heart" (1 Sam. 13:14). Throughout his life, he turned—and returned—to God as his refuge. No matter how far David strayed or how desperate he felt, the source of his strength and hope was no secret. His soul had found its true resting place. God alone was his salvation, rock, and fortress, and so he had peace.

When we try to find safety and security in earthly things, our frantic efforts not only leave us exhausted and fearful but are also doomed to fail. We will discover unshakeable protection and true rest in God alone. Only resting in God frees us from the tyranny of putting our souls' worth in anything, or anyone, else.

Reflect: God promises to assuage your fears with his perfect love and to provide all that you need.

Act: We need daily reminders of where our souls find their true rest. Try to begin each day with prayer and reflection as you quiet both your body and your mind. Notice what difference this makes as you move through your daily tasks.

DAY 10

Living within Our Limits

Lord, you have assigned me my portion and my cup; you have made my lot secure. The boundary lines have fallen for me in pleasant places; surely I have a delightful inheritance. (Ps. 16:5–6 NIV)

HARVEY KNOWS HIS wife would love for him to get home by 7 p.m. to have dinner with the family, but he keeps picking up new projects at work that demand more and more of his time. Clara likes to help her friends, but recently she's been taking on way too much responsibility for their lives. Jeremy has been trying to keep up with others in his social circle, but his expenses are out of control. Bethany nearly fell asleep at the wheel two days ago; she's been getting just three or four hours of sleep each night and eating poorly, caught up in binge-watching the latest season of her favorite show.

What do these men and women have in common? They are exhausted, stressed, and on the precipice of burnout. Why? Because they are straining against their limits.

We are creatures, not the Creator, and that means we come with limitations. Unlike God, we don't have unlimited resources. Unlike God, we're not omniscient, omnipotent, or omnipresent. Moreover, each of us is limited in different ways. Some of us need more sleep than others in order to function well; others seem able to juggle myriad responsibilities without overextending themselves.

It's difficult to see your limited resources and finite nature as delightful or pleasant. So how can the psalmist come to such a conclusion about his own "boundary lines"? He is at rest with what the Lord has given him, and he feels secure in the lot apportioned to him because it's guarded and assigned by the Lord himself. The psalmist doesn't try to be God; he is content in being the creature dependent on the Creator. What he has is assigned by God; and God himself guards his inheritance so that it is secure—it won't be taken away or stolen.

Rest is living within the limits God has assigned. We will never find real rest, physically or spiritually, if we try to live outside the boundaries God has assigned to us as his creatures. Just as Adam and Eve sought to "be like God" as the serpent promised (Gen. 3:5), we too often doubt the limitations God has assigned us, with painful consequences. Rest comes as we accept our God-assigned limitations, trusting that they will be good and even pleasant and delightful as we live within them.

Reflect: Which physical limitations bother you the most? Consider how much sleep you need, how much energy you bring to each day, and how many daily tasks or responsibilities you're typically able to accomplish well. How could accepting these God-ordained limits as "pleasant" and "delightful" help you to rest?

Act: Ask the Lord to give you wisdom about how to live with the limitations he's assigned you and to rest in him as God rather than trying to be God!

HOW TO REST

DAY 11

Sleep

*It is in vain that you rise up early and go late to rest, eating the bread
of anxious toil; for he gives to his beloved sleep. (Ps. 127:2)*

PSALM 127 TELLS us that we labor in vain unless it is the
Lord who "builds the house" and "watches over the city" (v. 1).
Substitute these phrases with your own examples: "Unless the
Lord _____ [raises my kids, provides for my family,
studies for college, homeschools, nurses, teaches Sunday school,
counsels, leads the company, cares for aging parents], those who
_____ [insert your work here] labor in vain." We know
our labor is in vain when we are anxious, feeling as if we never
have enough time in a day for the tasks we must accomplish. Our
sleep often suffers as a result. How easy it is for us to get caught in
a cycle of sacrificing our own sleep in our anxious toil!

I experienced this for myself when I began struggling with
insomnia during my sophomore year of college. Anxiety weighed
down my heart and soul as I wondered whether I was doing enough
for God. I was trying to keep up with academically challenging
courses along with rigorous standards I'd set for myself of reading
the Bible, praying, and mentoring younger women. In addition, I
was part of a student group that led tour groups and hosted pro-
spective students for our admissions department. Upon reflection,
I can easily see that I was exhausted and overwhelmed. My days
were full and busy, and so were my mind and soul as I tried to keep
up with what I thought God required of me. I consistently got to
bed late and awoke early, often with little restful sleep in between.
Like the psalmist, I was "eating the bread of anxious toil."

The Lord promises to give sleep to his beloved. Pause for a
moment with this truth. Sleep is a gift. It's a gift from the Lord.

And the Lord gives us sleep out of his love for us. He knows our tendencies to overdo and outdo and even try to be "god" in our spheres of responsibility. As we anxiously march on our nonstop treadmills, he reminds us that he's the one who keeps the world spinning on its axis. He's the one who cares for his people 24/7 because he does not need sleep (see Ps. 121). But *we* need sleep. And we are free to sleep because God the Creator keeps the world spinning while we do.

Whatever our work is, it is essential for us to make time for a good night's sleep. Sleeping is an act of faith. We can stop our work and sleep because God never does. We are finite; he is infinite.

One important disclaimer is that not *all* sleep problems have spiritual causes. There are many non-spiritual reasons for sleep disruption, including inconsolable infants, certain medications, chronic pain, and hormonal imbalances. Seek appropriate medical support and treatment, knowing that the Lord does not love you any less even as you struggle with sleep. He tenderly is with you through the watches of the night, especially when you feel alone.

Reflect: What do you tend to lose sleep over? Think about this literally: What tasks occupy your too-late nights or too-early mornings? What would it look like for you to entrust these tasks or concerns to the Lord?

Act: Set an alarm for *bedtime* seven to eight hours prior to your scheduled wake time, and notice how much more rested you feel after a few days. Consider adhering to your bedtime as an act of faith in the Lord's gift of sleep for you, allowing what's undone from the day to wait until the next morning.

DAY 12

Come to Jesus

"Come to me, all who labor and are heavy laden, and I will give you rest. Take my yoke upon you, and learn from me, for I am gentle and lowly in heart, and you will find rest for your souls." (Matt. 11:28–29)

WHAT BURDENS ARE you carrying today? Where do you feel the weight of the world? Perhaps it's the relentless pressure of meeting your children's seemingly infinite needs. Maybe it's your demanding boss at work or your own internal demands to achieve. Maybe it's the unpaid bills that are piling up, the taxes that are due, the aging parents who need your care, the heavy and uncertain future. Or maybe it's your own physical ailments or emotional anguish. Most likely, your burdens include the weight of determining which tasks to address first and how to find strength to keep bearing up under your heavy load.

Into this reality of the human condition, to those weighed down with sin and never-ending labor, Jesus speaks a welcome invitation: "Come to me." Laying down your burdens begins with coming to the only person who is strong enough to carry *all* that weighs you down. Jesus is God made flesh, fully human and fully divine. As a human being, he knows what it is to be heavy laden in a fallen world. As God, he has infinite strength and limitless resources to take on whatever weighs you down.

Where do you go first when you're feeling weighed down with the pressures of your life? Often we turn to books or magazines that offer us tricks for simplifying our schedules, organizing our homes, and better parenting our children. Sometimes we find the people to whom we can complain and receive empathy in return. Or we may try to escape our burdens entirely through numbing activities or addictions. But Jesus invites us to receive what our hearts need most. He alone offers soul rest.

Notice the progression in his invitation. First, Jesus asks us to come to him. Next, he promises rest. Then he tells us how to rest: by exchanging our heavy yokes for his and by learning from the one who is gentle and humble of heart. Finally, Jesus reiterates what we will find when we come to him: soul rest.

In the next reading, we will focus on Jesus's easy yoke and light burden. Today, our focus is on *coming* to Jesus. Start by noticing and naming the other invitations that are competing with this one. To whom or to what are you going for rest other than Jesus? What have those things promised? Have they ever delivered? Anyone or thing other than Jesus will leave with you *more* burdens, *more* labor, *more* demands and expectations. Only Jesus *gives* rest. It's not earned or deserved—it's a gift. We receive this gift when we answer his invitation to come to him with our burdens.

Reflect: As Jesus's disciple, Peter heard Jesus's invitation and seems to be echoing it in his first epistle when he encourages us, "Give all your worries and cares to God, for he cares about you" (1 Peter 5:7 NLT). What worries, cares, and burdens can you bring to God in prayer today?

Act: What other invitations are competing with Jesus's? Write them down and confess to the Lord that you need him most.

Act: Throughout your day today, as you notice the burdens in your labor, turn to Jesus in prayer as you remember his promised gift of rest.

DAY 13

Learn from Jesus's Easy Yoke

"For my yoke is easy, and my burden is light." (Matt. 11:30)

A YOKE IS a bar that joins two animals together to haul a load. It makes their work easier because their burden is now shared.[1] When we answer Jesus's invitation to come to him and accept his gift of rest, he offers us a yoke and a lesson. But it's not a lesson like those we're taught in school. Rather, we learn this lesson as we are yoked to walk alongside him and study his heart. It's relational.

The yoke Jesus gives us is different from the yokes we take on ourselves or have put on us by others. It is "easy." Jesus is not a demanding taskmaster. He isn't the boss who urges us to complete an unreachable deadline or the coach who pushes us beyond the breaking point. He's not the impossible-to-please parent or professor. With gentleness and humility, he offers to teach us a different way of living and working. He does not *demand* that we lay down our burdens, but he *invites* us to do so. As we walk alongside him, bearing his yoke of kindness and gentleness, we find rest for our souls.

When we are close to burnout, we often develop a skewed view of God. We feel beholden to many tasks and people, and in a combination of pride and exhaustion, we may not go to Jesus to find rest because we mistakenly believe he will only add to our burdens. We push through physical and emotional depletion, perpetually running on empty. In that state, it's easy for us to blame those around us for burdens we were never meant to carry alone. Our problem is that we have taken on much more than the easy yoke found in relationship with a gentle and lowly Jesus. To see Jesus more clearly, we must give up carrying everything we thought only we could bear. His heart is gentle toward us always, though we may be blind to this fact for a long time.

God the Son knows our limitations and burdens, and as we walk closely with him, we learn how and when to say yes and no with courage and clarity. As we experience what it feels like for him to bear our burdens, we learn how to bear others' burdens in partnership with him. As we're guided by his wisdom, we're also better able to discern which burdens are not ours to carry and which responsibilities are not part of the light burden he's given us. When we are yoked to Jesus, our souls know rest because they know him.

Reflect: How is Jesus's offered yoke different from the burdens you tend to carry?

Act: What do you need to say no to in your life so that you can say yes to Jesus's invitation to learn from him and find rest for your soul? If you are not sure what to turn down, ask a wise believer for help.

DAY 14

Repent of Unbelief

To whom did [God] swear that they would not enter his rest,
but to those who were disobedient? So we see that they were
unable to enter because of unbelief. (Heb. 3:18–19)

OUR VERSES FOR today are chilling, to be honest. We've been
studying the goodness of God's rest. We've seen that God provides refreshing soul rest for his people and invites us to lay down
our burdens. Now we come to a passage in Hebrews that says
God has promised that some will *not* enter his rest. The reason?
Their unbelief.

The author of Hebrews uses the Israelites as a case study. God
had miraculously rescued them from captivity in Egypt. After
a series of increasingly horrific plagues, Pharaoh begged Moses
to take his people and go. They fled into the desert, only to be
pursued by the Egyptian army. God miraculously parted the Red
Sea—the Israelites crossed safely to the other side, and the Egyp-
tians who pursued them were destroyed. Soon after, the Israelites rebelled. They complained about the lack of dietary variety,
even as God in his kindness provided them with bread and quail.
They began to view their captivity as preferable to freedom. They
chronically grumbled against God's leader, Moses. Consequently,
God kept an entire generation of Israelites from entering the
promised land or enjoying his promised gift of rest. Their disobedience, which was fueled by their unbelief in God's promises,
resulted in forty years of wilderness wandering before they died.

It is good to be sobered by this warning in Hebrews. And yet
there's an encouragement here too. Once we are united to Christ
by faith, the Holy Spirit empowers us to fight our own unbelief.
He reminds us that we belong to God—not because of what

we've done but because of the *finished* work of Jesus Christ for us. The way to experience and enter into true soul rest is to believe Jesus has accomplished everything necessary for us to enjoy it.

The Israelites who complained in the wilderness had miracles, promises, and laws intended to bring them to faith in the Messiah. You have the finished work of Christ to trust in. What is keeping you from believing that Jesus has accomplished everything necessary so that you can rest? As we close, consider these specific untruths, each of which indicates a measure of unbelief that hinders rest:

- I am indispensable, so I can't afford to stop working. (God won't provide.)
- If I cease from my activity, I'll have to face issues in my heart that I'd rather ignore and that God can't handle. (My sin and struggles are too big for God.)
- I won't be professionally or personally successful if I take time off. (My value comes from work instead of my identity as God's beloved child by grace through my faith in Christ's life, death, and resurrection.)
- I don't have value if I haven't accomplished anything by the end of the day. (Accomplishment is a visible result of my own effort; God is not always working in the unseen, eternal realm to accomplish his purposes, regardless of what I do.)

Reflect: Unbelief hinders us from embracing and experiencing God's rest. Which of the lies above resonates most with you? Can you think of others?

Act: Take a step of faith and set aside a period of time this week for rest.

DAY 15

Turn from False Gods

"They had rejected my regulations, refused to follow my decrees, and violated my Sabbath days. Their hearts were given to their idols. . . . 'I am the LORD your God,' I told them. 'Follow my decrees, pay attention to my regulations, and keep my Sabbath days holy, for they are a sign to remind you that I am the LORD your God.'" (Ezek. 20:16, 19–20 NLT)

WE HAD HINDU NEIGHBORS when I was growing up, and I was fascinated as well as discomfited and confused by the small statues scattered throughout their home. My parents explained that these were their idols, and they were a substitute for the true God of the Bible. If my neighbors came to know Jesus, they would have no further need for these idols. Since I didn't have any household idols, I mentally shelved idolatry as a sin struggle I didn't have.

Years later, in my early twenties, I learned about "idols of the heart." Pastor and author Tim Keller defined an idol as "anything more important to you than God, anything that absorbs your heart and imagination more than God, anything you seek to give you what only God can give."[1] An idol is anything that you put in the center of your life and heart, displacing God as what's functionally controlling you, and to which you give allegiance and priority.

Are you obsessed with gaining approval, comfort, or control? Does your work, image, family, or property absorb your imagination more than God? When you give more of your attention, time, and effort to your idols than to the Lord your God, you'll find it impossible to rest. An idol never says you've done enough but always demands more. When you're serving work and achievement, you can't ever take a break. If you try, you'll feel plagued by all the tasks you haven't done and all the goals you haven't reached. If you're worshipping your image, you might justify squeezing in a few more hours of shopping so that you can have "that perfect outfit." When you've overly valued your limited ability to meet needs, you'll have a hard time leaving emails, calls, or texts unanswered during hours, days, or seasons of rest.

Maybe you still aren't sure which idols occupy your heart. Well, what keeps you from observing Sabbath-day rest? God's words in today's passage warn that we violate the Sabbath when our hearts worship something or someone other than him.

On the Sabbath day, the Lord calls us to worship the true God, the one who alone satisfies our hearts' deepest desires and answers our souls' longing for rest. He tells us to shelve our idols of choice and remember that he alone gives to his beloved people what our idols falsely promise and can never deliver.

Reflect: Consider the last time you didn't honor a Sabbath rest. What idols got in the way of your rest?

Act: Dare to practice Sabbath-day rest this week as an act of courageous defiance of the idols that tempt your heart to false worship. Reflect on how God is better than these idols.

DAY 16

Remember the Futility
of Earthly Toil

What do people get for all the toil and anxious striving
with which they labor under the sun? All their days their
work is grief and pain; even at night their minds do not rest.
This too is meaningless. (Eccl. 2:22–23 NIV 2011)

THE AUTHOR OF ECCLESIASTES systematically examines
the major ways people pursue meaning in life "under the sun": by
acquiring knowledge, pursuing self-indulgent pleasure, living well,
and working hard. In today's passage, he concludes that earthly toil
is futile. It's quite a grim description: work brings pain, grief, and a
mental restlessness that interferes with sleep. Earlier, he points out
that we don't even know who will inherit all our hard-earned riches
after we die (see Eccl. 2:18–19). Indeed, work seems meaningless.

Today's passage elaborates on the pain and frustration that
permeated Adam's work after sin shattered paradise (see Gen.
3:17–19). Our work on this side of heaven won't bring us true
fulfillment and is fraught with futility. And isn't it also true that
our earthly work is what most often robs us of rest? Whether
we're answering that one last email before bedtime or cleaning
the house so it's spotless before guests arrive, work's demands
bring grief and pain. You may succeed in getting to "inbox zero"
before vacation, but tackling an overflowing inbox will be one of
your first tasks when you return. The sparkling home accumulates
dust, dirt, and discarded toys, clothes, books, and snacks. So why
do we build our lives around work's never-ending demands?

We forget the truth Ecclesiastes proclaims: without God, toil
is meaningless. *With* God, our toil has purpose. In contrast to

those who want us to work nonstop, constantly producing more and more, our Creator invites his people to work hard, recognizing that we work for him (see Col. 3:23), and then to rest.

Practicing rest is a way to defy the insidious temptation to worship our work. This may very well mean that we will have unfinished tasks at the end of a day, week, or season as we step into intentional rest. Perhaps you could have revised a paper more intensively before turning it in; perhaps you could have studied for a test for a few more hours. If you're a caregiver, you may need to entrust those in your care to someone else, engaging in planning and effort in order to be able to rest.

Work's demands during times of rest will rarely be fully silenced, but this is why we *practice* rest. We say yes to God's invitation for us to rest, to lay aside the futility and frustration of earthly toil as we entrust him with what remains incomplete or imperfect. And then we reengage work from a renewed perspective after our seasons of rest—forming our lives around God's priorities instead of work's never-ceasing demands for more.

Reflect: What demands does your work place on you? How has your work encouraged anxious striving and kept you from rest?

Act: How can you step away from work for a period of rest today or later this week? Make rest your goal, with the intention of putting your work in perspective and quieting its demands.

DAY 17

Refuse Swift Horses

"In repentance and rest is your salvation, in quietness and trust is your strength, but you would have none of it. You said, 'No, we will flee on horses.' Therefore you will flee! You said, 'We will ride off on swift horses.' Therefore your pursuers will be swift!" (Isa. 30:15–16 NIV)

TODAY'S PASSAGE CONJURES images of stubborn toddlers when they're told that it's nap time. They're having way too much fun, and their growing independence motivates them to say no. They don't have the perspective of their parents, who know that they will be exhausted and cranky if they don't have a midday nap.

Rest feels inefficient. It is counterintuitive to our mentality of productivity and achievement, which began for many of us when we started getting grades in school and competing with siblings for our parents' attention. Yet in God's economy, repentance, rest, quietness, and trust are more valuable than striving to achieve. It's countercultural for us now, and it was countercultural for the Israelites too.

In the context for today's verses, we learn that the Israelites are surrounded by enemies and once more on the verge of captivity. Isaiah the prophet tells them they will be saved by repenting and resting in God; they will find strength in quietness and trust.

Their response? They outright refuse to depend on God. His battle strategy feels unfamiliar—almost illogical—so they decide to trust in what they can *see* instead of resting in who God *is*. Like us, they want to think they have infinite wisdom and godlike strength rather than accept their finite and dependent nature as humans created by God.

"Nope. We choose our swift horses," they boast. So God steps back and says, "Fine. Let's see how well that goes for you."

Quite frankly, the horses seem to be the better option. Except . . . the passage suggests that their choice is not going to save them as they hoped, since it ends with the warning that their pursuers will be swift. Yes, they might feel like they've chosen wisely as they gallop away with the rush of wind on their faces, but their enemies' horses will soon catch up.

What "swift horses" do you prefer over the Lord's promised means? When it comes to rest, these are the strategies you think will refresh you without God's involvement. Perhaps it's a method for cleaning out and organizing your home. Or a new app for time and task management. Maybe it's working longer hours to get that promotion at work and the sense of financial security that comes with it. Many of us make a certain person our "swift horse" (mentor, spouse, child, parent, counselor, friend, and so on), craving the peace of their presence rather than the Lord's.

Some alternative options will always seem more immediately available, efficient, and effective than resting in the Lord. And God allows us to refuse his rest. But he doesn't leave us in that state, as we will see in tomorrow's reading.

Reflect: What "swift horses" have you chosen to rely on in the past? What happened?

Act: Take a moment to repent of your "swift horses" and reaffirm your trust in the Lord rather than in your own efforts.

DAY 18

Remember God's Compassion

*Yet the LORD longs to be gracious to you; he rises to
show you compassion. (Isa. 30:18 NIV)*

ONCE AGAIN, SHEILA had chosen busyness, an overly full
schedule, and saying yes to every request—and her soul felt it. She
noticed an unsettledness in her spirit that she couldn't pinpoint.
When she interacted with the women in her Bible study, she
noticed how emotionally detached she had become from them.
Sure, she knew that the burdens the other women shared at prayer
time were sad, and she could visually match their happiness and
excitement when good things were happening in their lives. But
she couldn't directly access any genuine grief or joy for them.

Then Sheila had an unexpected surgery. In the white space
of time and solitude as she convalesced, God's still, small voice
became louder. And she heard not his reprimand but his kindness. He had seen her exhaustion, and he had been gracious to
her. His promise had prevailed over Sheila's lengthy refusal of rest.

Take some time to think about this further: The Lord's deep
desire is to be *gracious* to you. What moves him to action is his
compassion. Even when we ignore or outright refuse his invitation
to rest, God's posture toward us as his children remains gracious
and compassionate. Like the father who welcomed his returning
prodigal by running toward him (see Luke 15:11–32), so God
rises in compassion for his harried and exhausted people and
greets them with welcoming grace.

What keeps us from returning to him sooner? Often it is our
skewed view of God's character. We assume that he is waiting
to shame and punish us. Instead, he is *longing*—it is his heart's

strong desire—to be gracious to us. He's looking for us to return to the rest he's prepared for us.

Even when we initially refuse to come to God and look to "swift horses" to save us instead, we cannot outrun the Lord's grace toward us as his beloved children in Christ. This grace may take surprising forms, as it did when Sheila's surgery forced her to slow down. Maybe it's a gap in your schedule. Maybe it's a friend's offer to babysit. Maybe it's a rainy day that makes yardwork impossible. Maybe it's an unexpected early morning that gives you more time to pray or prepare for the day. Where have you seen God's grace in your life recently? The opportunities that he gives you to rest are gracious gifts from a gracious Father. He wants you to take hold of them with hopeful expectancy and trust. What's keeping you from doing so?

Reflect: Think of a time when the Lord unexpectedly offered you a chance to rest. What did you do with that opportunity, and why? Looking back, is there anything you would have done differently?

Act: Take the next opportunity your schedule affords—whether that comes through unexpectedly long waits in a doctor's office, canceled meetings, or even a traffic standstill during a commute or a carpool—and seek to rest in the Lord with quietness and trust by reflecting on his character and promises. Notice how your heart, mind, and body respond as you sit in his compassionate presence.

DAY 19

Remember the Lord's Goodness

*How kind the LORD is! How good he is! So merciful,
this God of ours!... Let my soul be at rest again, for the
LORD has been good to me. (Ps. 116:5, 7 NLT)*

HOW DO YOU feel about camping? Many people love roughing it in the wild, but I just don't trust the tent to protect me from wild animals and extreme weather. Any time I spend the night in nature, my mind stays alert and my body vigilant to each suspicious sound. I end up barely sleeping at all.

It's hard to be at rest when you're afraid. How well do you sleep when you're dreading tomorrow? How much peace do you experience in the presence of people who have hurt you or whose disapproval you fear? How relaxed are you when unpaid bills keep adding up?

When we are frightened, today's psalm invites us to take our gaze away from the things that scare us and to consider the character of God. Our Lord is not only kind but also good. And he's not only good but also merciful. To top it all off, he's been good to you and me! The psalmist's joy crescendos in these verses as he reflects on the Lord's goodness to him.

Why is it so important to remember God's goodness? One obvious answer is that, as we live in a broken world, we are daily bombarded with so much that is *not* good. We must be intentional to call to mind the goodness of our God. Unlike human rulers, he always acts rightly and rules with justice. We can trust he will provide for us out of his abundant goodness. Because God's nature is good—perfectly holy—he will not hurt or betray us. Because he is good, he is strong enough to handle what confronts us.

Maybe as you read this psalm you feel pulled in a thousand different directions, acutely aware of the limitations that keep you from accomplishing all that is asked of you. Perhaps you feel anxious and afraid, wondering how you can deal with the challenges that you face. But as you redirect your attention to God, your soul can exhale at last. Nothing further is asked of you than to notice and celebrate his goodness.

And when you do, what relief follows! God has provided for your deepest needs through the life, death, and resurrection of Jesus Christ. Moreover, out of his goodness, he continues to provide abundantly for you in untold other ways. Whenever you feel frightened and anxious as you journey through this broken world, remind yourself, like the psalmist, of the Lord's goodness and be at peace again.

Reflect: Think of a recent time you saw the Lord's kindness, mercy, and goodness to you. In what way does that sign of his goodness help you to rest?

Act: For the next week, make a list of where you notice God's kindness, mercy, and goodness in your life. When you return to this list, use it as a reminder to your soul to be at rest.

DAY 20

Trust in God's Provision

*"Tomorrow is a day of solemn rest, a holy Sabbath to the LORD. . . ." So
they laid [the manna] aside till the morning, as Moses commanded them,
and it did not stink, and there were no worms in it. . . . And the LORD
said to Moses, ". . . . The LORD has given you the Sabbath; therefore on
the sixth day he gives you bread for two days." (Ex. 16:23–24, 28–29)*

HAVE YOU EVER told yourself, "God could rest because he's
God, and he was *finished* with the work of creation *before* he took
a day of rest"? According to this logic, it's easy to put off rest until
next week, when we'll be finished with a certain work project. Or
next month, when we've completed a busy holiday or sports season. Or maybe next year, when we'll be done with our big move
or out of a particularly busy stage of parenting. What's problem-
atic is that we will never be finished with all our tasks or work
before God calls us to eternal glory. While there may be pauses
along the way, our work and parenting and ministry will always
be in some state of incompletion.

In today's reading, we see God provide a double portion
of manna for the Israelites so that they can rest on the Sabbath.
Manna from heaven was God's people's only source of food in the
desert; they were dependent on his daily provision of this bread.
On the sixth day, the Lord told them to gather twice as much as
usual. He explained why: he would provide double, and the left-
over was for the Sabbath so that they wouldn't have to work. It
was the only day that manna stored properly until the next day,
and the Sabbath was the only day new manna did not fall from
heaven. Some did not gather extra ahead of time, and when they
went out as usual to get their manna on the Sabbath morning,

it wasn't there. They had refused to obey God, even though his command was a *gift* to them.

I wonder if this is why so few of us regularly engage in a day of rest: we don't believe that God will provide all we need in the other six days of the week. As we practice trusting God enough to step away from our work, even when it's unfinished, we develop an attitude of trust for all of life.

But when we don't trust God enough to practice a Sabbath rest, doubt in his provision shows up throughout our week as well. Workaholism often stems from the lie that no one is looking out for us and we won't ever have "enough." We end up exhausted and burned out because we aren't enjoying the Sabbath day as the gift it is intended to be to our hearts, minds, bodies, and relationships. And it's a gift we get to enjoy out of faith that God will provide even (and especially) for what lies unfinished.

Reflect: If you took a day for Sabbath rest this week, what would likely remain unfinished or incomplete? Consider if God's abundant provision for you might allow you to leave those things incomplete this week, entrusting the results of your work, ministry, or schoolwork to him.

Act: What are some choices you could make earlier in the week to protect and prioritize Sabbath rest as God's gift to you? Is there a day this week when you might need to "gather twice as much" so that you can rest on Sunday?

DAY 21

Cultivate a Posture of Humility

O LORD, *my heart is not lifted up; my eyes are not raised too*
high; I do not occupy myself with things too great and too
marvelous for me. But I have calmed and quieted my soul, like
a weaned child with its mother. . . . O Israel, hope in the LORD
from this time forth and forevermore. (Ps. 131:1–3)

HUMILITY IS ALL about where you're putting your hope. Are
you ultimately hoping in yourself—your abilities, your strengths,
your talents or gifts? A humble posture, which is necessary for
true rest, rises from a heart that recognizes its dependence on the
Lord, not self. If you happen to drift toward self-sufficiency, this
is hard to hear. It means that part of our own struggle with rest is
often a struggle with pride.

In Psalm 131 a calm and quiet soul is compared to "a weaned
child with its mother." Consider the difference between a nursing
baby and a weaned child. Nursing babies see their moms as the
source of every meal, and so they are rarely satisfied to be snug-
gled close to their mothers unless they've been fed already. Hungry infants are certainly neither calm nor quiet. However, once
these same children are fed or weaned, they can be at peace.

The psalmist is saying that he has quieted and calmed his
own soul to be at peace like that weaned child. How has he done
so? Look at how this psalm begins—with humility. The psalmist has not lifted up his heart or raised his eyes too high in pride.
He hasn't tried to do more than what the Lord has assigned to
him (see day 10). He has fed himself with hope in the Lord rather
than with hope in himself. He's well fed and satisfied, not anxiously living and searching for sustenance anywhere he can find it.

When we come to God through prayer and his Word, we hear the loud cries of our souls. We'll hear our souls' complaints and disappointments throughout our attempts at self-sufficiency. What's transformative is knowing that God hears all this too and has the power to satisfy our souls' deepest needs. It is his ability to quiet and calm our souls that allows us to refuse grasping the power that a sinful, prideful heart demands.

This may look like turning to God in prayer rather than reaching for our phones, food, or other activities and substances that (falsely) promise to calm our souls' clamoring. It may mean that we don't vent our frustration to a spouse or colleague before pouring out our hearts before God and seeking consolation through Scripture. It could look like refusing to assert our rights or to defend our position as we follow Christ to the low place and allow God to be our Defender (see Phil. 2:1–11).

God has already provided abundantly for our deepest need through Jesus, and therefore he will not spare us anything else that we truly need (see Rom. 8:32). A soul satisfied in the riches God gives is a soul at rest.

Reflect: Are there any areas of your life in which you are putting your hope in yourself instead of God? What are ways that you can calm and quiet your clamoring soul?

Act: If you notice your soul's loud cries today, practice crying out to God instead of looking to your own self-made solutions or resources.

DAY 22

Be Still

*"Be still, and know that I am God. I will be exalted among
the nations, I will be exalted in the earth!" (Ps. 46:10)*

STILLNESS IS UNNERVING. Some think of an invitation to
stillness as an invitation to reflect the calm serenity of a smooth-
as-glass body of water. But then I do it. I carve out the hours or
the days, and I make arrangements for the kids and the dog and
the job so that I can slip away for a quiet retreat. And about an
hour into the "retreat," I don't know what to do with myself.

Can you relate? Stillness feels oppressive if your inner critic
is berating you for what you're not doing or leaving undone. The
insecurities we try to manage through all our activity, achieve-
ments, pursuits, and relationships will often resurge in full force
in moments of stillness. Today's verse is a command that our
souls and bodies resist, yet desperately need.

Stillness of body and soul helps us to remember that God is
God and we are not. We cannot keep away our insecurities or banish the shame we feel when we stop all our "doing." Stillness forces
us to grapple with the reality that even our best efforts fall short
of salvation. Our hardest work does not move the needle of our
worth in God's sight (although we may settle for a fleeting sense
of people's approval). Our greatest accomplishments are power-
less to achieve the beloved identity our souls desire. Being still
and quiet before God awakens us to our own powerlessness—the
grief and helplessness we disguise through activity—and also to
God's eternal, infinite, and sovereign power.

The only worthwhile response to our powerlessness is to pray
and worship. As we quiet our minds and bodies, we awaken to
God's presence and power. He is active even when we are still. His

activity never ceases, and he will accomplish his goals—nothing short of being exalted among all people.

How can our suffering possibly be part of God's good purpose? Is our way hidden from the Lord? Does he see our disappointments and betrayals? We become like Job, our questions silenced by the power of who God is: "I know that you can do all things, and that no purpose of yours can be thwarted" (Job 42:2). We can be comforted by God's love like the prophet Zephaniah, who sings, "The LORD your God is with you, he is mighty to save. He will take great delight in you, he will quiet you with his love, he will rejoice over you with singing" (Zeph. 3:17 NIV).

In quieting ourselves before God, we realize anew that our activity doesn't earn or diminish his love for us. In bringing stillness to mind and body, we find the space to pray honestly and the strength to surrender what we cannot change. One translation (NASB) says, "Cease striving" in place of "Be still," and that alone says it all. Our striving is both *what hinders* our stillness and *why we need* the stillness of regular rest and retreat.

Reflect: When has stillness awakened you to a deeper knowledge of God's power and purposes? How does ceasing from your own activity and striving help to remind you that you are not God?

Act: Carve out at least ten minutes today to be still. Sit comfortably in a quiet room and close your eyes. Notice what emotions or thoughts arise. Bring these to God through prayer and worship him as you acknowledge that he is God and you are not.

WHERE TO REST

DAY 23

Rest in Green Pastures

*The Lord is my shepherd; I shall not want. He makes
me lie down in green pastures. (Ps. 23:1–2)*

M Y K N O W L E D G E O F S H E E P is limited to those I saw dotting
the lush countryside during the summer I spent in Ireland. That
summer I experienced multiple "sheep jams," which is what happens when sheep crowd a road, loudly bleating, and won't move.
A shepherd must come and lead them to safety.

Psalm 23 reminds us that we have a shepherd, and he is good.
Unlike the bad shepherds we may have experienced, whether in
our churches or our families, the Lord doesn't prey on his sheep
but lays down his life for them (see John 10:11). He is the shepherd who protects his sheep—who not only knows them by
name but also cares for them and provides for them. We "shall not
want" because of our shepherd, and Psalm 23 goes on to detail
what this means.

A sheep won't lie down and rest if it's starving and ill-treated
but will frantically consume any patch of green grass it sees. It
won't lie down until it is free not only from hunger but also from
fear, from conflict with other sheep, and from pests.[1] It means a lot,
then, for sheep to lie down—rather than feast—in green pastures.

No matter what your life looks like right now, know that the
Lord has brought you into green pastures. His perfect love is
powerful enough to banish all fear (see 1 John 4:18). His peace
breaks down walls of hostility that divide you from others (see
Eph. 2:14–16). He has defeated your worst enemy, Satan himself (see Rom. 16:20). He gives you the living water and bread
your soul needs. Knowing all that, can you trust him enough to
"lie down"?

Psalm 23 invites you to rest wherever your good, kind, all-providing Shepherd has led you. As you seek his goodness and meditate on his loving-kindness toward you, you can turn to him for the fresh grace that you need to be at peace. Rest in his presence, knowing he never leaves you. He is protecting you and providing for you even now.

Reflect: What specifically do you need to remember about the Lord's provision for you so that you can "lie down" in the pasture where you find yourself?

Act: In situations that are anxiety-provoking for you today, picture the Lord watchfully protecting you and call to mind his strength as your ever-vigilant and ever-providing Good Shepherd.

DAY 24

Rest beside Still Waters

He leads me beside still waters. He restores my soul. (Ps. 23:2–3)

THIRSTY SHEEP ARE RESTLESS SHEEP.[1] Once led to clean water, they rest after their thirst is satisfied. In today's passage, we see a beautiful promise: "He restores my soul." Not only does our Good Shepherd provide for our physical needs, but he also restores our souls. Where? Beside "still waters."

Still waters are "quiet and gentle waters, running in small and shallow channels." They are able to quench a sheep's thirst without posing any danger. Commentator Joseph Benson contrasts them with "great rivers, which both affright the sheep with their great noise, and expose them to be carried away by their swift and violent streams."[2] Nor are these waters dirty, threatening to sicken the sheep who drink from them. Likewise, God our Shepherd provides refreshing streams for our soul-thirst, but too often we're drawn to the dangerous waters that promise satisfaction yet end in destruction. Sin mimics and distorts the refreshment God gives, offering what will only harm us and leave us thirstier than before.

The psalmist David, the shepherd boy turned king, intimately knew the danger of straying to the wrong waters. When his sinful desires led him to sleep with his neighbor Uriah's wife, Bathsheba, he also arranged Uriah's murder in an attempt to get him out of the way. God sent the prophet Nathan to awaken David from his soul's sinful stupor.

Our sinful desires may not always be as obvious as David's, but they are just as destructive. Desires unchecked by the Holy Spirit will lead us astray, to waters that should make us afraid because they're dangerous to us. Having left the waters of true satisfaction in search of inferior things, we drink from whatever water source seems most obvious or convenient rather than wait to be led to the clean waters that will restore our souls.

How often we seek to provide for our own wants and needs apart from the provision and direction of the Lord our Good Shepherd! We settle for the momentary pleasure of an addictive substance or foolish activity rather than pursue real-life relationships that could bring connection and comfort. We isolate ourselves after betrayal or loss instead of seeking healing for our pain and grief through counseling and community. We overwork because of financial anxiety instead of asking for help or cultivating contentment.

Yet the Lord in his kindness brings us back. He is the shepherd who seeks and finds the lost and wandering (see Luke 15:3–7). He himself is the Living Water, as Jesus proclaimed when speaking to a Samaritan woman with a thirsty soul (see John 4:10–14). With the Holy Spirit living within us as a never-ending source of satisfaction, we will never thirst again (see John 4:14). God himself quenches our souls' thirst with his clean, peaceful streams.

A soul that drinks from still and living water is a soul at rest. This is both a promise and an invitation. Let us go to God with our thirst, forsaking the waters that have left us unsatisfied. The Good Shepherd will lead us to the waters of true soul restoration.

Reflect: Where have you sought to satisfy your desires and meet your needs apart from God? What would it look like for you to turn to God to satisfy your soul's desires today?

Act: Often allowing the Lord to shepherd and lead us means waiting for him to provide what will truly satisfy instead of reaching for what seems easiest and most convenient. What are some areas in your life in which God is asking you to wait on him?

DAY 25

Rest in God's Good Ways

Thus says the LORD: "Stand by the roads, and look, and ask for the ancient paths, where the good way is; and walk in it, and find rest for your souls. But they said, 'We will not walk in it.'" (Jer. 6:16)

IMAGINE THAT YOU'RE hiking in the woods on a new, unfamiliar trail. Now the path diverges ahead of you, and you have a decision to make: one path or the other. But you're not sure which one leads to the summit you're seeking. If, at that moment, a seasoned hiker comes along and tells you which path to take, won't you heed that direction?

In today's verse, the prophet Jeremiah describes how the people of Judah foolishly refused to walk in the good way that would bring them soul rest. Instead of obeying God and heeding his commands, they ignored and rejected God's Word (see Jer. 6:19) and pursued all kinds of evil. Jeremiah warned that their sin would have devastating consequences.

Sin often seems easier and more gratifying than obedience. We ignore the suffering of a neighbor because we have other places to be. We cheat on our taxes to enjoy some extra income. We pursue experiences that feel good, even if they're illicit. We go along with practices and policies that violate our consciences. We fail to see that the consequences of these actions and inactions will not lead to ease and gratification but to trouble and pain.

Only the path of Spirit-led obedience will yield the soul rest we're longing for. Consider the fruit of the Spirit: love, joy, peace, patience, kindness, goodness, faithfulness, gentleness, and self-control (see Gal. 5:22–23). When our lives are characterized by these qualities in increasing measure, our souls are at peace because we're living according to who we were created to be as God's own people, with the life of Christ displayed through us.

We have many opportunities to choose what steps to take next in our lives. The Lord invites us to stand, to look, to ask where the good way is—and then to walk in it and find rest for our souls.

Too often you and I respond to God's invitation the way Judah did. We stand at the crossroads, ask God for wisdom, and then refuse to walk in the good way of Spirit-led obedience. For some of us (myself included), we're too busy running and rushing to even recognize that we've come to a crossroads that requires a thoughtful choice.

Sometimes this refusal is outright and obvious, like that of Judah in Jeremiah's time, but more often it's subtle. It's the press of our to-do list, the fear of displeasing or disappointing other people, and our fierce commitment to the myth of our indispensability that lead us down the path of sin and human self-sufficiency. When we're walking (or running) on this path away from rest, we're busy with the wrong things and focused on the wrong audience. A marker that we've missed the good path will be that God feels distant and sin feels close. Turn to the Lord in repentance, as you turn away from sin and self-sufficiency. He leads us back to the ancient, better path of Spirit-dependency, where we will find rest for our souls.

Reflect: What attempts at self-sufficiency do you need to repent of?

Reflect: When has following the path of sin taken away your soul's rest?

Act: What's one choice you could make today to follow the Lord's leading into the path of Spirit-dependent rest?

DAY 26

Rest at Jesus's Feet

*Mary . . . sat at the Lord's feet and listened to his teaching. But Martha
. . . went up to him and said, ". . . Tell her then to help me." But the Lord
answered her, "Martha, Martha, you are anxious and troubled about
many things, but one thing is necessary. Mary has chosen the good
portion, which will not be taken away from her." (Luke 10:39–42)*

FOR ME AS a mother of twin daughters, the scene in today's
reading feels very familiar. I'm often brought in as an unbiased
third party whenever my daughters are in conflict. Each one
assumes I'll be on her side, or else she wouldn't ask me to mediate
in the first place. She wants me to be the authority who vindicates
her perspective.

As you picture this passage, put yourself in Martha's shoes.
She and Mary are offering hospitality to Jesus, their most important dinner guest, and Martha wants everything to be perfect.
She's bustling around with all the preparations necessary for such
a meal, and she's doing all these tasks alone while her sister is
deeply listening at the feet of Jesus. We would likely be frustrated
too. And we, like Martha, would appeal to Jesus, expecting him to
quickly send Mary back to assist us: "Lord, don't you care that my
sister has left me to do the work by myself? Tell her to help me!"
(Luke 10:40 NIV).

But Jesus surprises us by gently rebuking Martha and praising
Mary. Mary has chosen "the good portion," which is also trans-
lated as "what is better" (NIV). What she has learned from listening to Jesus will outlast the details of serving that are consuming
Martha. The food will be eaten; the table linens will eventually
fade; all the dirt she's banished will find its way back to the well-
swept corners and spotless counters.

When we take time to sit and listen at Jesus's feet, through his Word and in prayer, pausing from our labors and service, our hearts are reset. We are able to slow down and consider what our work and service is—and what it isn't. We remember what fuels all true service: receiving Jesus's love for us and allowing that love to flow through us toward the broken places in our homes, neighborhoods, churches, workplaces, and cities. Where do we rest? Not in our own efforts or distracted service, but in being with Jesus and allowing him to direct us to and empower us for the work he has for us.

Reflect: Describe a recent time when your service became a distraction from your relationship with Jesus. Think about a time when you were simultaneously consumed with anxious thoughts and full of criticism for others who weren't serving, working, or ministering as hard as you were.

Act: Before your next act of service, pause in reflection and prayer to listen to Jesus's words for your own heart.

DAY 27

Rest in Grace

I have been crucified with Christ. It is no longer I who live, but Christ who lives in me. And the life I now live in the flesh I live by faith in the Son of God, who loved me and gave himself for me. I do not nullify the grace of God, for if righteousness were through the law, then Christ died for no purpose. (Gal. 2:20–21)

DURING THE SUMMER between my sophomore and junior years of college, I first understood today's passage as an invitation to grace. As the "good girl" who was trying to please everyone, I had come to the brink of a breakdown fueled by anxiety and insomnia. On top of seeking to excel in difficult college courses, I was also trying to justify myself before God through tireless personal discipleship and evangelism. By the end of my sophomore year, I was exhausted and desperate. I needed to be set free from my ceaseless striving.

I will always remember that summer with affection as the "summer of grace." During that season, today's two verses from Galatians jumped off the page and into my heart by the power of the Holy Spirit. I felt free. Free from trying to do the impossible: work my way into holiness through keeping the law. In fact, I realized that my self-justifying efforts had been essentially proclaiming that Christ's life and death weren't necessary. I had been inadvertently nullifying God's grace.

To nullify God's grace is to negate it. When we do good works because we are striving for acceptance rather than trusting Christ's finished work, we are seeking to establish our own righteousness apart from God's grace. This is living out of unbelief—and it is exhausting and unfruitful. To rest in grace means looking to Jesus throughout the day in order to give up our own striving and trust in the sufficient grace we find in his life, death, and resurrection. Resting in grace is the practice of remembering God's love for us in Christ that motivated his sacrifice on our behalf.

Are you seeking righteousness through the law? How do you know? There are a thousand "laws" that we make for ourselves to give us a sense of rightness. Maybe you can't rest until your house is clean or all your emails are answered. Perhaps you base your worth on how well-behaved your children are or how much admiration you receive at work. Without first resting in Christ's work on your behalf, you will never be able to rest amid the unfinished and incomplete work of this life.

Reflect: What would it mean for you to rest because Christ's work on the cross is finished?

Reflect: When have you felt the futility of trying to attain your own righteousness? Consider some of the ways you've tried to fulfill God's law through your own effort. What would it look like for you to rest in Christ's finished work on your behalf instead?

Act: Take a moment now to turn to Christ in faith, remembering and thanking him for his loving sacrifice for you.

DAY 28

Rest in Quiet Trust

This is what the Sovereign Lord, the Holy One of Israel,
says: "In repentance and rest is your salvation, in quietness
and trust is your strength." (Isa. 30:15 NIV)

ONE OF MY DAUGHTERS practices ballet almost every day of the week. Why? Because she wants to become a strong ballerina, and that requires increased and intentional training. It's similar for any other pursuit. To become a strong writer requires more writing. Helping my daughters become strong readers required hours of toiling through books like *Bake, Mice, Bake!* Gaining strength in a certain area means applying more effort, more time, more focus.

But when it comes to spiritual strength, God turns this paradigm upside down. He tells his people that we find our strength when we rest—meaning that we grow spiritually strong as we cease *our* doing and rest in what *God* has done. To be strong in the Lord is to pursue quietness of soul and a posture of trust. In humility, we must acknowledge God as sovereign, entrust what we don't understand to his divine wisdom, and believe the desires of our hearts will be satisfied by his goodness. We cultivate spiritual strength by repenting of our sinful weakness and resting in *God's* strength.

We've seen that observing the Sabbath day is a good start—the Sabbath is a necessary corrective to our tendency to become work-obsessed and self-sufficient. The Sabbath reminds us that even as we pause our work one day out of seven, God is still at work to accomplish his sovereign purposes in our lives and our world. We pursue spiritual strength on the Sabbath as we gather with God's people to worship him, confess our faith, and participate in communion and fellowship.

But we don't build up spiritual strength only on Sundays. Daily prayer is another way to cultivate quiet trust in God as we bring our burdens to him. As we read Scripture, we receive fresh reminders of his love.

Earlier in our devotional, we saw that it's hard to remain open to resting in God. "Swift horses" are so appealing and offer an immediate sense of relief. There's something satisfying about marking items off a to-do list or completing a project. In a culture that idolizes productivity, nothing feels weaker than intentionally resting from our labors.

The beautiful reality is that spiritual rest is always available to us, and God strengthens us as we repent, rest, quiet ourselves, and trust him. All we need to do is stop, turn to God, find the strength of perfect love our hearts crave. Even if it's only ten minutes of turning away from our harried pace of busy nonstop activity to be quiet with the Lord in prayer or to meditate on a promise from Scripture, this is the place of rest: quietness and trust.

Reflect: How would you describe your current heart posture? Do you have an attitude of dependent trust in God, bowing in humble submission to his goodness and sovereignty? Or is your heart proud and defiant, standing in opposition to God as you depend on your own efforts to obtain what you think you need for life?

Act: Take ten minutes to cease from your activities and focus on God's activity in your life. Ask God to bring you back to this posture of quietness and trust throughout your day as your source of spiritual strength.

DAY 29

Rest in God's Love

"As the Father has loved me, so have I loved you. Abide in my love. If you keep my commandments, you will abide in my love, just as I have kept my Father's commandments and abide in his love. These things I have spoken to you, that my joy may be in you, and that your joy may be full." (John 15:9–11)

THIS WORD *ABIDE* is worth examining closely in our quest for rest. Where are we invited to abide—to dwell and not leave? It is no less than in God the Father's love. God invites us, his people, to make ourselves at home in his love, to rest in the identity made possible by Jesus Christ: we are beloved children of God. At rest in God's love, our true home, we will bear spiritual fruit and be filled with joy.

In college, I had a friend who was full of joy and exuded a supernatural, authentic love for others. I often wondered how she lived this way. One year, a group of us visited her parents on spring break, and it all made sense. I saw how much her parents loved her—lavishly, generously, without reserve—and they invited us into their love because we were her friends. My friend grew up in a rich soil of love, and this naturally produced a life of joyful ministry.

The best human loves can only palely reflect the love of God. The way a mom feels about her newborn baby? Multiply that by infinity, and you're barely coming close to the way God loves you. The way a groom delights in his bride? Amplify it by infinity, and that's merely a taste of God's love for you. The joyful companionship of lifelong friends who've shared both weeping and laughter? Compound it by infinity, erasing all hints of misunderstanding or disappointment, and you're only beginning to see God's perfect love for you.

Consider the commandment we've studied throughout this devotional: Sabbath rest. What results from obeying this command? One day a week, we have a specific time to rest and be refreshed as we rest, which in turn increases our physical and spiritual enjoyment of life.

To rest in God's love yields joy. If your joy's running low, consider your practices of rest. Are you getting enough sleep? Remember that sleep is important—a gift from the Lord to his beloved (see day 11). Is ministry overwhelming? Step away for a few hours or days for spiritual replenishment. Are you trying to win the love and approval of others? Sit at Jesus's feet as you read Scripture and pray, asking him to remind you of his perfect, never-ending love (see Eph. 3:14–19). As we become more deeply rooted in the rich soil of Christ's love, we find rest. As we abide here, we will find the love we seek, and we will be filled with joy.

Reflect: Another way to think of abiding in God's love is to "make your home in God's love." When have you felt the most deeply loved by God? What Scripture passages remind you of God's love for you?

Act: Throughout today, return to the thought "You are perfectly loved." Notice how comforting it is to know that you're loved even in your hardest moments or biggest failures today. Does this begin to lighten your disappointments or ease your loneliness?

DAY 30

Rest in the "Already and Not Yet"

So then, there remains a Sabbath rest for the people of God, for whoever has entered God's rest has also rested from his works as God did from his. (Heb. 4:9–10)

AS WE NEAR the end of our devotional, we come full circle in redemptive history. Today's verses remind us of the beginning of rest, when God himself rested on the seventh day of creation. Their reference to "Sabbath" calls to mind God's commandment to the newly rescued people of Israel during their exodus from Egypt to the promised land. But because this passage is written after the life, death, and resurrection of Jesus Christ, the author of Hebrews proclaims that *we* can experience God's rest in a true Sabbath rest yet to come.

One way to describe the era of redemptive history in which we live is the phrase *already and not yet*. We have *already* received the promised Messiah, and our salvation is secured, but we have *not yet* experienced the full restoration that Christ's resurrection set in motion for all creation. There is a fuller Sabbath rest yet to come.

Learning about and practicing all aspects of biblical rest—the Sabbath day, a posture of humility, soul repose in God, abiding in the love of Christ, mental and physical refreshment —is meant to root us more firmly in our current place in God's story of redemption. What this means is that *present* rest proclaims our *past* salvation as God's people through Christ along with our *future* hope of eternal rest with God in the new heavens and the new earth. Because of Christ, we who are united to him by faith go where he goes, and he opened the entrance for us into God's rest of salvation with his death and resurrection. It was a costly entrance fee, impossible for us to pay even with a lifetime of good works. But Christ covered it for us, proclaiming on the cross, "It is finished." Our entrance into God's rest is made possible by his grace, not our works.

Now the sweetness of a Sunday dinner with friends becomes a foretaste of the great heavenly wedding feast of God when he joins forever with the bride of Christ (see Rev. 19:6–8). The refreshment of a spiritual retreat whets our appetite for the time when we will be face-to-face with God for all eternity. The reprieve of a quiet hour alone in prayer and God's Word reminds us that our spiritual strength comes from the Lord, that Christ completed the necessary work to save us, and that one day we too will rest forever from all our earthly labors. When we are weary and burdened, turning to Jesus to lay our burdens at his feet in prayer and worship causes us to long for the day when he himself will wipe away every tear from our eyes (see Rev. 21:4). A night of peaceful sleep makes us grateful for our Creator and reminds us that we have God-given limits we should honor. Our present-day practice of rest is a way to enjoy the benefits of redemption Christ has *already* won for us, while also increasing our hope in the full restoration that we have *not yet* experienced but that awaits us in heaven with God.

Reflect: How can your practices of rest remind you of how God saved you?

Reflect: How can your practices of rest help to increase your hope and longing for the future eternal rest to come?

Act: Practice an aspect of rest this week that reminds you of how God has saved you or of what awaits you in heaven.

DAY 31

Rest in Heaven

*"It is done! I am the Alpha and the Omega, the beginning
and the end. To the thirsty I will give from the spring of
the water of life without payment." (Rev. 21:6)*

REVELATION 21 PROCLAIMS the joy of eternal rest that
springs from the completion of redemptive history. Jesus's words
on the cross, "It is finished!" are echoed here in victorious fulfillment: "It is done!"

All of history is moving toward the end of a world under
sin's curse and the beginning of a new, perfect kingdom made for
God's people to dwell in forever. There will be no fear of death,
no grief, no pain. No tears and no more losses. All thirst will be
satisfied in eternal springs of life untainted by sin's bitterness. God
will be the heart of this holy community—its very life and light
source. We will rest in his loving and good presence forever.

All our earthly rest is merely a foretaste of the eternal rest yet
to come. Our earthly rest will never be perfectly refreshing, nor
will we be able to banish the restlessness caused by sin's lingering
presence.

Consider the last time you went on a vacation. During your
travel, you likely encountered some unexpected delay or hassle,
whether it was a traffic jam on the highway or a flight that didn't
leave on time. You may have even experienced, as I have, a delay
that necessitated an overnight stay at a hotel along the route to
your final destination. As annoying as these inconveniences and
hassles were, didn't keeping your destination in mind help you to
endure the journey? You knew that once you arrived, you would
relax into your anticipated vacation.

It should be no different for us—we know that in the end, the troubles of this life will be redeemed and we'll rest for all eternity. We should live now with our eyes set on that final reality of a future rest.

As we observe the pattern, posture, and pace of rest in our present lives, we proclaim this eternal rest of the coming kingdom, where all earthly toil will be finished. None of the thorns and futility from work will remain, for the curse will be finally and completely reversed in the new Eden.

Our *present* rest builds our hope in the *future* rest God has prepared for his people. Rest restores our joy and fruitfulness. When we rest, we proclaim to a weary world that a day is coming when all striving will cease for those who have been saved by God's gift of grace through Jesus. Rest strengthens us for our work until Christ comes again.

Reflect: How can times of intentional rest increase your appetite for the eternal rest prepared for and awaiting God's people?

Act: As you think of earthly rest as an appetizer for the coming eternal feast, set aside regular times to rest and be refreshed in God. Look at your schedule for your day, week, month, and year, and ask God to help you to block out hours, days, and perhaps even extended seasons for the purpose of the holy pause of rest. Plan to engage in what will be physically and spiritually replenishing for you during these seasons of rest.

Conclusion

I've penned most of these meditations as the winter turned to spring. The seasonal change has reflected how my soul has come alive as I've rediscovered the joys of rest. There is so much more for me to learn, and there are so many ways for me to put into practice what we've thought about together. I don't want our journey together to come to an end.

I want to become more diligent and more joyful about regular weekly Sabbath in my family's life. I long for my too-busy, hustle-and-bustle pace of life to slow down to match the rhythms of a soul at rest in Jesus. I want my heart's posture to be one of worshipful rest as my soul is calmed and quieted in the presence of my Creator and Sustainer. My hope is to increase my daily practice of being still and silent so that I can hear and behold God's goodness and glory and activity in the world more clearly.

My prayer is that you too have been captured by Jesus's invitation to rest. As you've practiced rest while reading this devotional, I hope you've wanted to go deeper. I've included a list of a few books that I would recommend for further reading and study on this topic.

We have seen that rest is rooted in creation itself, as God our Creator instituted a "holy pause" after six days of work in Genesis. He later commanded Sabbath rest to remind the Israelites that he had freed them from slavery and set them apart to be his own people. Throughout the psalms and the prophets, we see that rest reflects the humble posture of a soul that is satisfied in the Lord's goodness and sovereignty.

When Jesus enters the scene, he shows us that Sabbath rest is not at odds with mercy and good works. He invites us to trade our burdens for his easy yoke, to sit at his feet like Mary, and to find strength for fruitful ministry as we abide in him. His cry on the cross of "It is finished!" echoes into eternity, freeing us by grace to rest because he has completed all the work of salvation. We will still labor for his kingdom, but we do so with a pattern of regular rest and a posture of dependence on Christ for strength. Our practice of rest in a fallen world points toward the day when we will enjoy God's presence perfectly and be freed from all sin and burdens forever. That will be true rest!

Expect to encounter much resistance as you seek to rest in Christ. The Enemy of our souls will do everything he can to distract us from finding true strength and restoration in God. I have to mentally set aside my to-do lists whenever I pray and read the Bible. I have to quiet the demands and expectations related to the roles and responsibilities I carry. Specifically, this means I usually have to ignore the unanswered emails, my phone alerts, the dishes, the piles of laundry, the books I should be reading, and the volunteer requests, so I can step away to be with the One who will provide for what is most needed. You may have to learn to be content with being less productive than your coworkers or fellow classmates because of your commitment to the Sabbath and to other periods of rest each week. But will it be worth it?

A thousand times yes! Rest is a gift of God to his people. That's what I'm leaning into and delighting in the more I practice rest. My weekly day of rest is one I look forward to, and so I make the necessary preparations in order to enjoy it. I've had to rearrange how and when I work. You probably will too, whatever your "work" in this season is. As you observe the Sabbath and find other times in your week to practice rest, take time to explore that which truly refreshes your soul. Is it reading a book in your backyard on a beautiful day? Or taking a hike? Or inviting people for a meal together?

I hope and pray that we will know more of the love, joy, and grace of God as we create space in our lives, schedules, and souls to rest and that our rest will become part of how we display the light of Christ to a weary world exhausted by never-ending toil and soul restlessness.

Consider these words from Jean Sophia Pigott as a guiding prayer as you move forward in your lifelong practice and pursuit of rest:

Jesus! I am resting, resting in the joy of what thou art;
I am finding out the greatness of thy loving heart.
Thou hast bid me gaze upon thee, and thy beauty fills my soul,
For, by thy transforming power, thou hast made me whole.

Ever lift thy face upon me, as I work and wait for thee;
Resting 'neath thy smile, Lord Jesus, earth's dark shadows flee.
Brightness of my Father's glory, Sunshine of my Father's face,
Keep me ever trusting, resting. Fill me with thy grace.[1]

Acknowledgments

I MUST BEGIN by thanking you, the reader, for considering my words. I hope my story of learning the rhythms of grace over and over finds resonance with you too.

I want to particularly thank my counselor, Sydney, who helped me to find soul rest and restoration after a season of depression and burnout left me utterly depleted. Your compassionate listening, compelling questions, and gentle truth-telling have led me back to Jesus's love as my resting place again and again. This book would not have been possible without the healing journey you've invited me to and accompanied me on.

I am grateful for the team at P&R Publishing, who has made this book what it is today. Thank you to Deepak Reju for giving me the opportunity to be included in this invaluable series and for your patience as you waited so long for me to follow up with you. I want to especially thank Amanda Martin and Joy Woo for their excellent editorial feedback and Dave Almack for championing this book from the beginning.

I have some amazing friends and neighbors who have heard versions of my musings on rest over the past several months. Thank you especially to Jeff and Katherine Donnithorne, who blessed and encouraged this work from its beginning; to Regan Bruckner, Conner Cochran, Ellen Dykas, Melissa Huff, and Sarah Warren, who read portions of the initial manuscript and gave invaluable feedback and encouragement; and to Cat, Katherine, Karen, Maria, Joy, the Hunter House girls, and the LBR group, who have been cheerleading supporters all throughout this writing journey. Y'all are the best, and I'm so grateful for you.

Thank you to my counseling colleagues at Mountain View Christian Counseling, who have encouraged me during this project, and to the pastoral staff and congregation at Mitchell Road Presbyterian Church, who have given me the opportunity to teach aspects of this book's material over the last year, helping me to sharpen and hone its content. I'm grateful to be in community with you as we learn together how to rest in grace while sharing the love of Christ with a hurting world.

I'm thankful for my husband, Seth, and twin daughters, Lucia and Alethia, who patiently allowed me to write another book (knowing it would mean a more distracted wife and mom at times!) and cheered me along with their unwavering love and support.

And most of all, I give glory and eternal gratitude to the God who has lavished the gift of his love to me, that I might rest in it—no matter how many times I escape into the hustle of "swift horses," your compassionate love pursues me and awaits me even there.

Notes

Day 2: Rest Is a Mark of Freedom
1. Sermon by Frank Hitchings, at Lookout Mountain Presbyterian Church in Lookout Mountain, Tennessee, as shared with me through the sermon notes of my dear friend Jen Schaefer in spring 2023.

Day 5: Sabbath Rest Is Refreshing
1. See *Merriam-Webster*, s.v. "refresh (*v.*)," accessed May 30, 2024, https://www.merriam-webster.com/dictionary/refresh.
2. I'm indebted to Jeff and Katherine Donnithorne and their Sunday school class at First Baptist Church in Montgomery, Alabama, for sharing this definition of *rest* with me.

Day 6: Sabbath Rest Is a Delight
1. Amy Carmichael, *God's Missionary* (repr., Fort Washington, PA: CLC Publications, 2010), 37.

Day 8: An Invitation to Busy Disciples
1. See "The Benefits of Napping," National Sleep Foundation, May 10, 2021, https://www.thensf.org/the-benefits-of-napping/.

Day 13: Learn from Jesus's Easy Yoke
1. See Brannon Deibert, "What Is Yoke in the Bible? Meaning of Jesus' Teaching," Christianity.com, updated April 23, 2024, https://www.christianity.com/jesus/life-of-jesus/teaching-and-messages/the-yoke-of-jesus-biblical-meaning-and-importance.html.

Day 15: Turn from False Gods
1. Timothy Keller, *Counterfeit Gods: The Empty Promises of Money, Sex, and Power, and the Only Hope That Matters* (repr., New York: Penguin Books, 2016), xvii–xix.

Day 23: Rest in Green Pastures
1. See W. Phillip Keller, *A Shepherd Looks at Psalm 23* (repr., Grand Rapids: Zondervan, 2007), 41–42.

Day 24: Rest beside Still Waters

1. See W. Phillip Keller, *A Shepherd Looks at Psalm 23* (repr., Grand Rapids: Zondervan, 2007), 57–59.
2. Benson Commentary, on Psalm 23:2, available online at Bible Hub, accessed July 1, 2024, https://biblehub.com/commentaries/psalms/23-2.htm.

Conclusion

1. Jean Sophia Pigott, "Jesus, I Am Resting, Resting," 1876.

Recommended Resources
for Growth

Barton, Ruth Haley. *Embracing Rhythms of Work and Rest: From Sabbath to Sabbatical and Back Again*. Downers Grove, IL: InterVarsity Press, 2022. [I loved this book's focus on the practicality as well as the necessity of Sabbath rest and sabbaticals. If you want to think through how to align your life with a regular pattern of weekly Sabbath and seasonal sabbaticals, this is a great book to use.]

Comer, John Mark. *The Ruthless Elimination of Hurry: How to Stay Emotionally Healthy and Spiritually Alive in the Chaos of the Modern World*. Colorado Springs: WaterBrook, 2019. [This book addresses a major barrier to rest in our busy lives: hurry. Comer is honest about his own struggles, and he gives hope as well as guidance for how to move from hurry to simplicity in the face of the demands of our families, communities, and churches.]

Dawn, Marva J. *The Sense of the Call: A Sabbath Way of Life for Those Who Serve God, the Church, and the World*. Grand Rapids: Eerdmans, 2006. [When I was in the midst of an overfull life of ministry, this book showed me another way of serving—out of the overflow of abiding with Jesus instead of out of exhaustion. It's not only for those in ministry vocations, since all Christians are called to serve one another in love.]

Huie, Eliza, and Esther Smith. *The Whole Life: 52 Weeks of Biblical Self-Care*. Greensboro, NC: New Growth Press, 2021. [In a year's worth of weekly devotional readings with suggested practices and thoughtful reflection questions, this book gives a gospel framework and practical suggestions for how to pursue spiritual, emotional, physical, and relational refreshment. I highly recommend this as a follow-up to this devotional as you seek to create space for rest in your life.]

BIBLICAL
COUNSELING
COALITION

The Biblical Counseling Coalition (BCC) is passionate about enhancing and advancing biblical counseling globally. We accomplish this through broadcasting, connecting, and collaborating.

Broadcasting promotes gospel-centered biblical counseling ministries and resources to bring hope and healing to hurting people around the world. We promote biblical counseling in a number of ways: through our *15:14* podcast, website (biblicalcounselingcoalition.org), partner ministry, conference attendance, and personal relationships.

Connecting biblical counselors and biblical counseling ministries is a central component of the BCC. The BCC was founded by leaders in the biblical counseling movement who saw the need for and the power behind building a strong global network of biblical counselors. We introduce individuals and ministries to one another to establish gospel-centered relationships.

Collaboration is the natural outgrowth of our connecting efforts. We truly believe that biblical counselors and ministries can accomplish more by working together. The BCC Confessional Statement, which is a clear and comprehensive definition of biblical counseling, was created through the cooperative effort of over thirty leading biblical counselors. The BCC has also published a three-part series of multi-contributor works that bring theological wisdom and practical expertise to pastors, church leaders, counseling practitioners, and students. Each year we are able to facilitate the production of numerous resources, including books, articles, videos, audio resources, and a host of other helps for biblical counselors. Working together allows us to provide robust resources and develop best practices in biblical counseling so that we can hone the ministry of soul care in the church.

To learn more about the BCC, visit biblicalcounselingcoalition.org.

Also from P&R Publishing

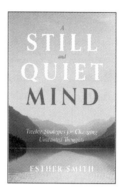

Are you distracted by racing or anxious thoughts? Distressed by intrusive or irrational thoughts? Struggling with sinful or untrue thoughts? You may feel trapped in your own head, but God and his Word have given you many different ways to find freedom.

In this practical and sympathetic guidebook, biblical counselor Esther Smith provides twelve powerful strategies that are targeted to different thought struggles. Each chapter is filled with a variety of exercises so that you can begin to change your thoughts right away and live at peace.

"Esther Smith has written the most practical and biblically faithful book on navigating unwanted thoughts that we have ever encountered."
—**David and Krista Dunham**, Counselors